THE LIGHT BEFORE CHRISTMAS

A FAMILY ADVENT DEVOTIONAL

BY MARTY MACHOWSKI

ILLUSTRATED BY SARAH BLAND-HALULKO

New Growth Press

New Growth Press, Greensboro, NC 27401
All Scripture quotations, unless otherwise indicated, are taken from the
ESV® Bible (The Holy Bible, English Standard Version®), copyright © 2001 by
Crossway, a publishing ministry of Good News Publishers. Used by permis-
sion. All rights reserved. ESV Text Edition: 2016.

Scripture quotations marked NIV are taken from the Holy Bible, New International Version®, NIV®. Copyright ©1973, 1978, 1984, 2011 by Biblica, Inc.™
Used by permission of Zondervan. All rights reserved worldwide. www.
zondervan.com The "NIV" and "New International Version" are trademarks
registered in the United States Patent and Trademark Office by Biblica, Inc.™

Illustrations: Sarah Bland-Halulko
Design/Typesetting: Alecia Sharp

ISBN 978-1-64507-292-8
Library of Congress Cataloging-in-Publication Data on file
LCCN 2022015602

Printed in India
29 28 27 26 25 24 23 22   1 2 3 4 5

CONTENTS

"THE PEOPLE WALKING
IN DARKNESS HAVE
SEEN A GREAT LIGHT;
ON THOSE LIVING IN
THE LAND OF DEEP
DARKNESS A LIGHT
HAS DAWNED."

ISAIAH 9:2 NIV

INTRODUCTION

The prophet Isaiah foretold of a day he would never see. A day when the light of God would pierce the darkness of the night sky and announce the coming of God's Son. Isaiah prophesied of that day to Israel saying, "The people walking in darkness have seen a great light; on those living in the land of deep darkness a light has dawned." So, long before the light of the star over Bethlehem shown bright, the prophets foretold the dawning of the light.

The Advent devotional you are about to read tells the story of the true Christmas light. From before the dawn of creation through the eternal light of God's glorious throne, God's light has always shone bright. Long before the twinkle of a star directed the wise men to Jesus, God planned to send his only son to rescue God's children from the darkness of sin and bring them all into the glorious light of his presence.

Light is the most amazing element of God's creation and people have long celebrated its beauty at Christmas time. Christmas lights decorate our windows and doorways, our houses, and trees. Though many have lost the meaning behind the light, they marvel at the twinkle of Christmas lights as they shine forth in the darkness in beautiful arrays of color. Children celebrate when they see a well-lit Christmas decoration and the lights of Christmas on a dark night cheer up the weariest soul.

Once you know the story of light and its place in the Christmas story, the lights that decorate homes at Christmas will bring a deeper joy to you. So read through these pages during the Advent season and take your family on a light filled journey through the Bible. Allow the Scriptures you read to warm your heart at the fire of God's amazing grace. Your children will look forward to reading the family Christmas story, "The Light Before Christmas," that marks the beginning of each week's devotion.

Read through a section of this book for each week of Advent. We've provided devotions, activities, and suggested prayers. Let the words of Isaiah's prophecy shine forth in your family—so that upon your family God's light may shine.

HOW TO USE THIS BOOK

This book includes thirteen family Advent devotionals—three for each of the four weeks of Advent and one more for Christmas. Over the course of Advent, you will learn what the Bible says about light and see how the theme of light weaves its way through the Christmas story and God's plan of salvation.

To plan your Advent celebration, after Thanksgiving look at the calendar and take note of the four Sundays before Christmas. These mark the start of the four weeks of Advent. There are three family Bible devotionals for each of these four weeks.

Prior to Advent, purchase an Advent wreath or the supplies to make your own following the instructions provided below. The Advent wreath consists of a simple circle of evergreens. It represents our hope of eternal life in Christ. The four outer candles mark the four Sundays of Advent. These four candles represent the light of God reaching the world through the birth of his son Jesus. In the center of the wreath is placed a fifth, larger, candle that represents the Savior, marking his place at the center of God's plan.

Beginning with the first Sunday of Advent, start your celebration by lighting the first Advent candle and reading the first chapter of the story, "The Light Before Christmas." In the week that follows, take your family through the three devotions provided for the week.

Each day's devotion starts with an opening activity. This may be an object lesson, a fun fact to explore, or a song to sing. In addition, there are four traditional Christmas hymns to learn and sing, one for each week of Advent. Close each devotional with prayer, and then have one of your children blow out the Advent wreath candle(s).

Follow the same pattern for each of the four weeks of Advent. On Christmas Eve, light all the Advent candles and read the closing chapter of "The Light Before Christmas" story. On Christmas Day, relight all the Advent candles, read the Christmas Scripture from Luke's gospel, and sing "Joy to the World."

MAKE AN
ADVENT WREATH

SUPPLIES:

* 96 inches (8 feet) evergreen roping—real or artificial
* 16-inch diameter green foam ring
* three 10-inch purple (or white) taper candles
* one 10-inch pink (or red) taper candle
* one 2-in x 6-in white pillar candle with holder or white jar candle.
* aluminum foil, heavy duty
* knife or apple corer
* hot glue gun

INSTRUCTIONS:

Lay the foam ring on a protected work surface. With the sharp knife or apple corer, cut out four holes in the ring equal distances apart to accept the four taper candles. Be careful to cut the holes slightly smaller than the candle diameter. Hot glue the candles into the holes making sure they are perfectly vertical. Wrap the evergreen roping along the foam ring, gluing it to the ring as you go. The 8-foot length should be plenty to cover the outer and inner circumferences of the foam ring. The goal is to cover the ring completely. Set the wreath on a table and place the pillar candle in the center. Remember to protect the surface of the table underneath the wreath from dripping wax.

LIGHT

Light the first Advent candle before

reading chapter one of "The Light

Before Christmas" story and before

beginning each day's devotion.

☆ 1 ☆

A VISIT WITH GRANDMA

J ust like on Christmases past, the little brick church on Maple Avenue was packed shoulder to shoulder with people. Joyful voices sang out—spilling into the streets and through the neighborhood. Long robes swayed as the choir danced and clapped their hands to the beat. Children and adults joined together in singing the season's first Christmas carols—welcoming the town to listen and sing along. Together they sang the words:

I once lived in darkness, deep as the night,
Then God sent his Spirit to open my eyes.
The Light of the World gave me back my sight.
All heaven rejoiced when I saw the light.

Shout joyful tidings, salvation has come,
The Light of Christmas in Bethlehem born.
The babe in a manger is God's only Son;
Good news of great joy, he is Christ the Lord.

Inside the sanctuary, on a wooden pew, sat eleven-year-old Mia with her grandmother. She was spending the entire month of December helping her grandma prepare for Christmas. Mia loved her grandmother very much and looked forward to their time together all year long. She was thrilled to leave her home in the south to enjoy the brisk snowy mountains.

Today was the first Sunday of Advent, and in several weeks, Mia's parents would join them for Christmas. As she listened to the melodious chorus of carols, she began humming along. Everything felt warm and festive—until she noticed tears on Grandma's face.

Mia listened more closely to the words of the song and realized it was about seeing the light—and of sight being restored. *How could they be so insensitive to Grandma's blindness*, thought Mia. *It's no wonder she's crying!* Mia put her arm around Grandma and hugged her gently. She was relieved when the song finally ended, and especially eager to walk back home for lunch. She tried to be patient while her grandmother greeted nearly every person in the church.

When they finally stepped outside, the bright sun forced Mia to squint. A warm glow shone on their faces, and the snow crunched under their boots. Mia's thick braids bobbed and bounced in the brisk air, as she walked to the beat of Grandma's long white and red cane tapping the sidewalk ahead. Though Grandma couldn't see the road before her, she knew exactly where they were going. But Mia wished her grandmother could appreciate the beautiful scene.

"Grandma," said Mia, "the town is all decorated for Christmas! The trees are covered in snow, it is all so beautiful."

"Yes, this is Doctor Jones's place," Grandma replied. "He always decorates his white fence with red ribbons, and they match the cardinal at his feeder." The spry woman lifted her cane and pointed right at the bird.

Mia was astonished. "How did you know that, Grandma?"

"I heard the flutter of his wings and the chirp of his call," she answered. "You can always tell a cardinal. I just guessed it was a bright red male to match the ribbon. Was I right?"

"Yes," Mia answered. "But how did you know this was Doctor Jones's place?"

"I count the steps. It's sixty-two paces from the church to Doc's place. He has been hanging red ribbons on his fence since before you were born. It's one of his Christmas traditions."

Then the cardinal danced on the branch of the pine, dusted the fence with snow, and called out a sharp high-pitched tweet.

"Cardinals must be so beautiful," Grandma remarked. "Everyone seems so excited to see them, especially in the snow."

Mia wished Grandma could see. Then she remembered the song—and Grandma's tears.

"I'm sorry about that song at church," said Mia. "They should have known it would hurt your feelings."

"Oh, I wasn't sad, dear! I actually love that song!" replied Grandma. "Pastor Jake knows it's one of my favorite carols. Those were happy tears!"

Mia pulled away, shocked. "But Grandma," she exclaimed, "The whole song is about being blind! How could that possibly make you happy!"

"I might be blind on the outside, but inside I can see." Grandma paused. She lifted her cane and pointed it right at the sun. "I might not be able to see the sun with my eyes, but I can feel its rays on my face. See how I can point it out to you?"

Mia nodded, "Uh-huh."

"Light is that strong, my dear. When sighted folk look up toward that sun, the brightness blinds them. Forces you all to close your eyes. But we all stand blind before the light. And there is no better season to celebrate the coming of God's light than at Christmastime. In the Bible, the prophet Isaiah says that all people walk in darkness until they see a great light—until a new light has dawned."

"I'm not sure I understand," replied Mia.

Grandma smiled. "Even though I was born blind, God opened the eyes of my heart to see him. While I might not be able to see the beautiful pine trees and the ribbons on the fence, I can see God and experience his light."

Mia still didn't quite understand, but she was relieved that Grandma was no longer crying.

Grandma then took Mia's hand and said, "I have a present for you—a special book I want us to read together to celebrate Advent. You can open it after lunch."

Mia beamed for she loved opening presents. "But, Grandma," she asked, "How are you going to read a book to me? Is it written in Braille? Is that why it's special?"

"Actually, you are going to read it to me!" said Grandma. "We'll enjoy it together—like I did with my father when I was your age, back when I was double blind."

"Double blind?" Mia asked, for she had never heard that term before.

"Yes, dear. I was blind on the outside and the inside. You see, inside we are all born blind. The eyes of our heart are blind with sin. But once God shines his light into our hearts, we can see. It was in listening to Daddy read that book, that God opened my eyes to first see the light."

Intrigued, Mia asked, "What's the book called?"

"You'll have to wait until after lunch," smiled Grandma. Then she led the way home, up the snow-covered path.

The two said nothing more. As they neared the house, Grandma tapped her cane on the front porch and lifted her foot right in time to take the first step up. It was as though her grandmother could see the steps in front of her. The weathered cedar planks filled the front porch with the familiar smell of Grandma's house, even in the cold. Mia stepped forward and pulled open the wooden screen door. The long spring screwed to the door broke the silence as it creaked and sounded their arrival. Grandma passed Mia the key, which she inserted into the center of the knob and turned, giving the door a shove. A burst of warm air greeted them as the two came in out of the cold. Mia took in a deep breath; she loved the smell of Grandma's house.

Inside, Mia helped set the table for lunch. As she did, her grandmother looked up and offered a silent prayer to heaven. Mia was so busy with the dishes, she didn't notice another tear roll down her grandmother's wrinkled cheek.

After lunch, Grandma invited Mia to open her present. They would read it together while enjoying a slice of apple pie. Grandma baked a pie each Saturday afternoon and Mia loved her pies! She wondered which would be better: the pie or the book. She noticed the book sitting nearby, wrapped in red paper with white snowflakes.

Mia wasted no time; she tore right through the wrapping paper and read aloud the book's title, *The Light Before Christmas*. The elegant letters surrounded an image of a beautiful starburst.

Mia gave her grandmother a big hug. "Thank you, Grandma!" she said. "I can't wait to begin!"

Grandma laughed. "Well, go on, let's do it!"

Mia flipped eagerly past the first few pages until she reached chapter one. She snuggled in close to Grandma and proceeded to read.

God Created Light

WARM-UP

SUPPLIES:

* A lamp with a clear bulb so you can see the filament or LED

Start by having everyone close their eyes. Ask them to imagine what it would be like to be blind like the grandmother in the story. Talk about the ways their life would change if they couldn't see. Have them open their eyes and discuss how it feels to see again.

READ THE WORD

And God said, "Let there be light," and there was light. And God saw that the light was good. And God separated the light from the darkness. God called the light Day, and the darkness he called Night. And there was evening and there was morning, the first day. Genesis 1:3-5

THINK ABOUT IT

Long before he made the earth, God lived in unapproachable light—a light so bright, no one could come near his throne (1 Timothy 6:16).

Then, according to his plan God created the earth out of nothing at all and left it floating in the darkness of space. It was into this darkness that God spoke his first command. His first words were, "Let there be light." The instant he finished, "there was light" (Genesis 1:3). The light of the world burst forth at his command. Then "God separated the light from the darkness" (Genesis 1:4).

Next God created the stars to shine bright light for all to see. God ordered them "to give light upon the earth" (Genesis 1:15). From the moment of God's command the stars lit up the sky. If you go outside on a clear night you can still see the very same stars he first created that day.

Then, God set a special star near the earth and he called it the "the greater light to rule the day" (Genesis 1:16). People have given our special star a name. We call it the sun and the light that shines out, we call sunshine and daylight. God placed the sun perfectly close to our planet. If the sun was much closer our world would heat up and the water turn to vapor; too far away and the oceans would freeze. But, by God's design he located our star just where it needed to be to provide light for the life he created and we now enjoy. Without light, everything we know would die.

When God was finished making the lights of the heavens he looked at all that he made "and God saw that it was good" (Genesis 1:18).

TALK ABOUT IT

God created the light by speaking it into being. God created trillions of stars and knows each one by name (Psalm 147:4). What does that kind of creative power teach us about our amazing God?

SING TOGETHER

The Christmas hymn "O Come, O Come, Immanuel" was first written in Latin and sung in the early 1700's. The word Immanuel means "God with us" and comes from Isaiah's amazing prophecy that foretold the coming of the Christ child: "Behold, the virgin shall conceive and bear a son, and shall call his name Immanuel" (Isaiah 7:14). Notice how verse six weaves the theme of light into the promise of hope of a coming Savior. Isaiah foretold of a bright morning star. Jesus said that he is the one Isaiah spoke of. Jesus said, "I am the root and the descendant of David, the bright morning star" (Revelation 22:16).

O Come, O Come, Immanuel   (verses 1 and 6)

VERSE 1
O come, O come, Immanuel,
and ransom captive Israel
that mourns in lonely exile here
until the Son of God appear.
Rejoice! Rejoice! Immanuel
shall come to you, O Israel.

VERSE 6
O come, O Bright and Morning Star,
and bring us comfort from afar!
Dispel the shadows of the night
and turn our darkness into light.
Rejoice! Rejoice! Immanuel
shall come to you, O Israel.

PRAY
Thank God for his amazing power and for creating light.

The Heavens Declare the Glory of God

WARM-UP

SUPPLIES:

* A picture of Michelangelo's sculpture, the *Pietà*. (Wikipedia has a good image.)

Display the picture of Michelangelo's famous sculpture, the *Pietà*. Introduce it by giving a little background: The sculpture was finished in 1499 and is on display at St. Peter's Cathedral in Rome, Italy. Point out how the sculptor made Mary's robes look soft and flowing even though they are made out of marble—and marble is a rock! Talk about the scene: Mary holding her dead son after he was taken down from the cross. Pietà means pity. Just as this wonderful sculpture points to Michelangelo's greatness, so the creation of the universe and the world around us showcase the greatness and glory of God.

READ THE WORD

The heavens declare the glory of God, and the sky above proclaims his handiwork. Day to day pours out speech, and night to night reveals knowledge. There is no speech, nor are there words, whose voice is not heard. Their voice goes out through all the earth, and their words to the end of the world. In them he has set a tent for the

*sun, which comes out like a bridegroom leaving his chamber, and,
like a strong man, runs its course with joy. Its rising is from the end of
the heavens, and its circuit to the end of them, and there is nothing
hidden from its heat.* Psalm 19:1-6

THINK ABOUT IT

Michelangelo is one of the greatest artists of all time. It only takes
one look at one of his magnificent paintings or sculptures to see that
Michelangelo was a master. His creative work shouts of his greatness without speaking a single word. In the same way, the creation
around us speaks out God's greatness for all to see. The Apostle
Paul said that God's creation tells all people that God is real and
that he is all powerful. We know this, Paul says, just by looking at the
things that God made (Romans 1:20).

Nothing speaks of God's greatness and glory like the stars in
the sky. The Bible tells us that the stars in the heavens "declare the
glory of God, and the sky above proclaims his handiwork" (Psalm
19:1). God's creation shouts of his greatness. Consider these amazing
facts. No one has ever been able to find the end of the heavens.
The further we look the more stars we see. The stars are grouped
into clusters called galaxies. Our galaxy is called the Milky Way and
it is made up of 100 billion stars. That's a lot of stars. If you counted
one star each second, it would take you more than 12,000 years
to count them all. But the Milky Way is only one galaxy. Scientists
estimate there are 100 billion galaxies. That means the universe has
more than 70 billion trillion stars—that's 10,000 stars for every grain
of sand on earth!

We can only guess at the number of the stars, but God knows
exactly how many there are. The Bible tells us that God "determines

the number of the stars; he gives to all of them their names" (Psalm 147:4). Isaiah wrote about God's creation of the stars:

> Lift up your eyes on high and see: who created these? He who brings out their host by number, calling them all by name; by the greatness of his might, and because he is strong in power, not one is missing. Isaiah 40:26

Now consider the light that shines from the stars. Light is super-fast. Light can travel from New York City to Hawaii in a split second. In fact, in the short amount of time it takes you to say the word "amazing," light can travel the whole way around the earth four times! Now that is amazing!

TALK ABOUT IT
What does the amazing beauty of the night sky with all the stars shining bright tell us about God?

SING TOGETHER
Sing this week's Christmas hymn, "O Come, O Come, Immanuel." (See p. 23.)

PRAY
Thank God for creating the stars and praise him for his wonderful works.

Two Kinds of Light

WARM-UP

SUPPLIES:

* objects for identifying (one for each participant)
* blindfold
* flashlight

Gather together and explain that you're going to play a guessing game. Blindfold a volunteer. Hand them an object (piece of fruit or a toy) and ask them to try to identify it just by feeling it. (No peeking allowed!) Give everyone who wants to try, a turn at guessing an object. Then talk about how much easier it is to know what something is when there is light to see.

If your children are older, do this activity after dark. Gather in a room and turn off the lights. Tell the children to follow you as you lead them around the room. Walk slowly and talk about how hard it is to see your way in the dark. Then turn the flashlight on and try the exercise again using the flashlight to light the way. Talk about how much easier it is to walk with the light to guide you.

READ THE WORD

How sweet are your words to my taste, sweeter than honey to my mouth! Through your precepts I get understanding; therefore I hate every false way. Your word is a lamp to my feet and a light to my path. Psalm 119:103–105

THINK ABOUT IT

The Bible talks about two kinds of light: physical light and spiritual light.

Physical light is the light that shines from the sun and the other stars. The light of the sun sustains all life. Without its light everything on earth would die. Physical light includes the red glow of a fire and the flash of lightning during a storm.

The Bible also talks about spiritual light. God's truth is described as a lamp that lights our way (Psalm 119:105). We see this light with the eyes of our heart. Just as the light of the sun pushes back the darkness so we can see our way, so the light of God's truth shines into the darkness to show us the way to God. Just as we cannot live without the light of the sun, we can't live without the light of God's Son, Jesus.

TALK ABOUT IT

How does God's Word light up our way and keep us from falling into sin?

SING TOGETHER

Sing this week's Christmas hymn, "O Come, O Come, Immanuel." (See p. 23.)

PRAY

Ask God to help you follow his Word so that you walk in the light of his truth and not in the darkness of sin.

DARKNESS

Light the first and second Advent

candles before reading chapter two

of "The Light Before Christmas" and

before each day's devotion.

☆ 2 ☆

PUSHING BACK
THE DARKNESS

As Mia hung the last strand of lights on the tree, she asked her grandmother, "Why do we hang lights on trees anyway?" Grandma responded, "Before electricity, many people lit their Christmas trees with candles. They were a symbol of Jesus being the light of the world. He came to shine light in darkness. But today, most folks decorate their trees with lights because they look so nice—and they're much safer than candles. "

Mia asked, "Grandma, what do you like most about Christmas trees?"

"Well, I especially love their sweet, rich scent! And you picked out a winner this year!" She paused then chuckled, "Well, except for that

one bare spot on the side. We might want to face that toward the wall."

Astonished, Mia exclaimed, "Wait! How did you know?"

"Remember, dear: sight isn't just with your eyes. You also see through touch. Go ahead, close your eyes and give it a try. Run your fingers along the tip of the needles. Notice the bare spot just down from the top."

Mia closed her eyes, reached for the branches, and gradually moved her hand from one side to the other. "I feel it! It's right here!" She opened her eyes and smiled. "I saw with my hands."

"See?" replied Grandma. "When I was a little girl, my daddy and I would walk down Main Street on Christmas Eve, and he would tell me all about the lights. He'd tell me which were red, green and blue and which were clear—which flashed and which stayed steady. And then he'd snuggle me close and kiss my cold cheeks until I laughed and laughed! Even though I've never seen Christmas lights with my eyes, I have experienced their beauty through others. Stringing my tree with lights welcomes back a flood of wonderful memories.

"Now, why don't you place the star at the top of the tree."

Mia picked up the decorative star from the end table. She asked, "Why does the star go at the top?"

"It reminds us of the star of Bethlehem, which led the wise men to Jesus. And it still points us to Jesus today. He's the bright morning star."

Mia set the star atop the tree. Perfect, she thought to herself. As she reached for the power cord, she remarked, "All finished! Can I plug it in?"

"Let's wait till later, when it's dark," replied Grandma. "My daddy always waited until evening so that when he turned on the tree, it lit up the room. He wanted the light beaming from the tree to push back the darkness, like Jesus came to push back the darkness and light the way to heaven."

Mia reluctantly set down the cord.

"The light of Jesus came into the world to shine in the darkness. The Bible says his light will not be overcome. That's actually what the next section in our book is about. Shall we continue?"

Mia retrieved the book from the shelf and began reading the next chapter, titled "Darkness."

Darkness

WARM-UP

SUPPLIES:

* bright flashlight or lamp; practice making hand shadow puppets
  (search online)

Shadows are created when something blocks the light from shining. During evening or in a darkened room, place the lamp or flashlight on a table next to a light-colored wall and use your hand to
cast a shadow. Move your fingers around to see all the different
funny shadows you can create. Demonstrate how to make the hand
shadow puppets you practiced.

   Then talk about how just as an object can block the light from
shining on the wall, so our sin can block the light from shining forth
in our lives.

READ THE WORD

*The way of the wicked is like deep darkness; they do not know over
what they stumble. Proverbs 4:19*

THINK ABOUT IT

Just as there are two kinds of light, there are two kinds of darkness.
When the sun sets at the end of the day, a physical darkness falls on
the earth. We call this darkness night. Unless there's a bright moon

we can barely see. There are places of deep darkness where even the light of the moon and stars cannot reach, like in a room with no windows or the pitch black of a cave.

While the physical darkness that falls on the earth can frighten us, there is a more terrible darkness, spiritual darkness. The Bible talks of the darkness of evil and sin that works to dim the spiritual light of God.

The darkness of sin first fell on the earth when Adam and Eve disobeyed God and ate the forbidden fruit. Solomon said, "The way of the wicked is like deep darkness; they do not know over what they stumble" (Proverbs 4:19). That was the day sin and death entered the world and spoiled God's beautiful creation. Now that the curse of darkness has come, all people are born with the darkness of unbelief in their hearts (Psalm 51:5), and the whole world is sick with the curse of evil (Romans 5:12). But there was one part of God's creation sin tried to overcome but could not—God's light. The whole reason we need Christmas is for the light of God to come to conquer the spiritual darkness that has invaded our world. Jesus came as a baby to defeat that darkness. One day all darkness will be overcome by the light of Jesus.

TALK ABOUT IT

The Bible tells us that God is light. Why do you think the Bible compares sin to darkness?

SING TOGETHER

The Christmas hymn for the week is "The First Noel." It was first sung in England 200 years ago. It tells the story of the angels appearing to the shepherds to announce the birth of Jesus, and the story of the wise men who followed the star. Notice the theme of light from the star in this song.

THE FIRST NOEL   (verses 1–3)

VERSE 1

The first Noel the angel did say
was to certain poor shepherds in fields as they lay;
in fields where they lay keeping their sheep,
on a cold winter's night that was so deep.

REFRAIN

Noel, Noel, Noel, Noel,
born is the King of Israel.

VERSE 2

They looked up and saw a star
shining in the east, beyond them far;
and to the earth it gave great light,
and so it continued both day and night. [Refrain]

VERSE 3

And by the light of that same star
three Wise Men came from country far;
to seek for a king was their intent,
and to follow the star wherever it went. [Refrain]

PRAY

Ask God to help you turn away from sin (darkness) and follow the
Light (Jesus).

Light Overcomes

WARM-UP
SUPPLIES:
* two flashlights or lamps
* coffee mug

Start in a darkened room by shining one flashlight at the mug to cast a shadow. Talk about how the cup is fighting against the light, casting a shadow. Then show how putting a second flashlight on the opposite side wins the battle against the shadow and overcomes the darkness. Now turn on the main light of the room to see how that overcomes the darkness in the room.

READ THE WORD
In the beginning was the Word, and the Word was with God, and the Word was God. He was in the beginning with God. All things were made through him, and without him was not any thing made that was made. In him was life, and the life was the light of men. The light shines in the darkness, and the darkness has not overcome it. John 1:1–5

THINK ABOUT IT
The Apostle John doesn't tell the Christmas story in his gospel in the

same way that Luke does. Luke tells the familiar story of the angels in the sky appearing to the shepherds in the fields to announce that the Savior had been born in Bethlehem. John describes Christmas a different way: as the arrival of the Light that comes to fight against the darkness.

Let's read it again. (Reread the passage above.)

Luke also spoke of the struggle between light and darkness in recording the words of Zechariah, the father of John the Baptist. John, born shortly before Jesus, was appointed by God to announce Jesus's ministry. This is what Zechariah said as he held his newborn son, John:

"And you, child, will be called the prophet of the Most High; for you will go before the Lord to prepare his ways, to give knowledge of salvation to his people in the forgiveness of their sins, because of the tender mercy of our God, whereby the sunrise shall visit us from on high to give light to those who sit in darkness and in the shadow of death, to guide our feet into the way of peace." Luke 1:76–79

No matter how hard the forces of evil try, they cannot overcome the Light. The truth of God's light will forever shine bright. Light always wins in a battle against darkness. Even if we light a lamp in a dark room, the light always wins and the darkness flees. Now of course our lightbulbs can burn out, or our batteries die and our flashlight go dim. But God is eternal and the Light of his glory never goes out.

TALK ABOUT IT

What happens to darkness when you turn on a flashlight? Which wins: the light or the darkness? Did you ever know a time when darkness swallowed up light? How does a flashlight pushing back the darkness remind us of God's victory over evil?

SING TOGETHER

Sing this week's Christmas hymn, "The First Noel." (See p. 38.)

PRAY

Ask God to fill you with the light of his truth and push back the darkness of sin from your life.

There Is No Darkness in God

WARM-UP

SUPPLIES:

* CD

* bright flashlight

* copy paper (one sheet for each person plus one extra)

* crayons or markers in all the colors of the rainbow

Look up pictures of rainbows on the internet to show your children just how beautiful they are. The colors in the rainbow are created when sunlight passes through water droplets and splits into different colors of light. You can create your own rainbow by spraying a fine mist of water with a hose on a sunny day or by shining light through a prism. But an easy way to see a rainbow is by observing how light reflects off the back of a CD.

Say: *Let's make our own rainbow—and then draw it. And remember, violet always bends the most and red the least.*

Hold up the CD and show the children the blank side. Ask the children to describe what they see. (Bands of shimmering color). Tilt the CD back and forth and show them how the colors shift and change. Then shine a flashlight at the CD. Hold a sheet of white paper so the light reflecting off the CD shines onto the paper. The reflected light will make a rainbow on the paper.

Pass out the art supplies and color rainbows together.

READ THE WORD

God is light, and in him is no darkness at all. 1 John 1:5

THINK ABOUT IT

The Bible tells us that "God is light, and in him is no darkness at all" (1 John 1:5). The Bible also tells us that God covers himself with "light as with a garment" (Psalm 104:2) and God lives in "unapproachable light" (1 Timothy 6:16). That is a light so bright that no one can look upon it or come near. The sun that shines on our earth is like that. The sun is so bright it will blind your eyes. That is why we are taught to never look straight at the sun. The light of the sun is also unapproachable. This means it is so hot that anything that tries to come close burns to nothing. Now the light of God is brighter than the sun. God's light would consume the sun.

Though no one has ever seen God face to face, God opened the heavens and allowed Ezekiel to catch a glimpse of heaven. This is how he described what he saw,

> "High above on the throne was a figure like that of a man. I saw that from what appeared to be his waist up he looked like glowing metal, as if full of fire, and that from there down he looked like fire; and brilliant light surrounded him. Like the appearance of a rainbow in the clouds on a rainy day, so was the radiance around him." Ezekiel 1:26–28 NIV

God gave Noah the rainbow to remind him and everyone who came after him of his promise to never destroy the earth by flood again. God made a way to ensure Jesus could be born as a far-off grandson of Noah. It was Jesus who brought the salvation the ark of

Noah represented. Noah and his family survived the storm of God's judgment inside the safety of the ark. We can ride out the storm of God's final judgment by trusting in Jesus. Jesus is our ark.

So, whenever we see God's rainbow in the sky we should think of Christmas, the day God sent his only son Jesus, born as a babe in a manger. All those who believe are safe "in Christ" and will one day see the rainbow of light shooting from his throne. The Apostle John was given a vision of God on his throne and wrote it down in the book of Revelation. He too describes the colors of the rainbow shining from the throne of God: "And the one who sat there had the appearance of jasper and ruby. A rainbow that shone like an emerald encircled the throne" (Revelation 4:3 NIV).

TALK ABOUT IT
Why should rainbows remind us of Christmas?

SING TOGETHER
Sing this week's Christmas hymn, "The First Noel." (See p. 38.)

PRAY
Thank God that he is perfect light and he has allowed his Word to teach us about his light.

RESCUE

Light the first, second, and third Advent

candles before reading chapter

three of "The Light Before Christmas"

and before each day's devotion.

✩ 3 ✩

RAINBOWS

Two Sundays later, as they gathered to read after lunch, Mia asked, "Grandma, who helps you make pies when I'm not here?"

"Well, I'm grateful to have wonderful friends! Most Saturday afternoons they come to help."

"What about the other times?" Mia asked.

"I can make a pie by myself, if that's what you're asking," chuckled Grandma.

"I did kind of wonder . . . but just a little," confessed Mia.

"Think about the first time you tried typing on your keyboard," began Grandma. "You likely had to look down at each key you touched. You probably typed so slow—click, click, click—until it became more familiar. But now, I hear you typing! You are fast! And I'd imagine you're no longer looking down at those keys! When I made my first pie, I felt lost. It took a lot of time and focus, but now it's second nature. I can peel an apple like a dream, crimp a piecrust

in my sleep, and turn the controls of my oven like a safecracker, all by feel."

"But how do you know the pie is done?"

"Why the smell of the pie crust browning and the sound of the filling bubbling tells me the pie is done."

"You're amazing, Grandma," Mia remarked.

"Speaking of amazing, I think rainbows are amazing," said Grandma "I haven't been able to stop thinking about them since we read our last chapter."

"Oh yeah?" Mia asked.

"Yes, if there was one thing on earth I'd really like to see, it's a rainbow. Have you ever seen one?"

"Yes! I saw one last year after a storm."

"Tell me, Mia, what was it like?"

Mia tried to think of how to best describe it to Grandma—without colors and without seeing, but with something she could picture in her mind. She continued, "I think it's like eating a fruit salad—the taste of blueberries mixed with honeydew, strawberries, and watermelon. Blend all those flavors together in your mouth and that is what a rainbow looks like with your eyes."

Grandma smiled and said, "That's perfect. I can almost taste it!" She continued, "To satisfy my curiosity I've read about rainbows. And I've read about how the eye sees color.

"The eye has three types of color sensors; one type for red light, another for green, and a third for blue light. These three primary colors of light blend together to create all the colors of the rainbow.

"Sunlight (white light) is made up of all the colors we see. Each color has its own amount of energy. So when the white light of the sun shines through droplets of rain in a passing storm, the white light splits into colors and each color bends a certain amount depending on its energy. That's why a rainbow bends and that's why violet always bends the most and red the least.

"And here is the most amazing part! If you shine red, green, and blue lights together, these three primary colors together produce white light!"

"I'm confused," said Mia. "The colored light shines white?"

"Yes! Think of the spotlights in a theater. If you focus red, green, and blue stage lights at the same spot, the three shining together make one bright white light. The three are one and the one is three. Each distinct color is equally light and equally powerful, but there are not three kinds of light, only one. It reminds me of the Trinity—of God being three in one—the Father, Son, and Holy Spirit."

"But I thought the primary colors were red, blue, and yellow, not red, blue, and green!" said Mia.

"The primary colors of the earth (paint) and those of light are different. The primary colors of the earth are yellow, red, and blue. If you mix those three together, like an artist does with their paint, it creates a muddy darkness. But when you mix the three colors of light—green, red, and blue—it shines one marvelous white light."

Grandma continued, "I believe that God designed light as a reflection of his beauty and wonder. One day, he will restore my vision and I will look upon his light with new eyes! Like Isaiah and John, I will look upon the rainbow of God's glory shining from the throne!"

"That explains why you love talking about light," said Mia.

"And especially the greatest light of all—Jesus! He is the Light of the World whom the Father sent to put an end to all darkness. But I'm getting ahead of myself. We better read our next chapter!"

Called out of Darkness

WARM-UP

SUPPLIES:

* Two clear glasses filled with water

* dark liquid food coloring (any color but yellow)

* a spoon

* a white sheet of paper

Fold the sheet of paper in half so that it can stand as a backdrop for the glass. Tell the children that the glass of water represents the world and the food coloring represents sin. Squirt a dozen drops of food dye into the spoon. Then say to your children, let's see what happened when sin entered the world. Then all at once, tip the spoon of coloring into the water and watch as the cloud of color spreads. Talk about how once sin entered the world, it affected the whole world. Come back to the glass at the end of the session. Compare the stained water to the second glass of clear water to see how the dye (sin) spread.

READ THE WORD

But you are a chosen people, a royal priesthood, a holy nation, God's special possession, that you may declare the praises of him who called you out of darkness into his wonderful light. Once you were not a people, but now you are the people of God; once you had not received mercy, but now you have received mercy. 1 Peter 2:9-10 NIV

THINK ABOUT IT

Ever since sin entered the world it spread to everyone and everything. Just within the first six chapters of Genesis sin spreads from Adam and Eve to infect everything:

> The LORD saw how great the wickedness of the human race had become on the earth, and that every inclination of the thoughts of the human heart was only evil all the time. Genesis 6:5 NIV

We are all born with a sinful love of darkness and a hatred for God's light. The Apostle Paul said that even though we could see God's glory in the wonders of creation, people became fools and "their foolish hearts were darkened." They traded God for idols. People rejected the light of God and loved the darkness instead of the light (Romans 1:21–23).

Job talked about the darkness of sin when he said, "In the dark, thieves break into houses, but by day they shut themselves in; they want nothing to do with the light. For all of them, midnight is their morning; they make friends with the terrors of darkness" (Job 24:16–17 NIV).

Today, people install motion detecting lights around the outside of their homes to ward off would-be burglars. The lights come on if anyone approaches. The Bible tells us why lights work to scare away criminals. "For everyone who does wicked things hates the light and does not come to the light, lest his works should be exposed" (John 3:20). While John is speaking of spiritual light and darkness, his statement is also true about physical light. Criminals love to do their evil deeds in darkness where they can work their evil in secret.

God could have crushed the darkness and judged all the people of the earth, but he had a plan to save his people and call them out of darkness back into his marvelous light (1 Peter 2:9). On the very first Christmas the angels proclaimed God's plan to the shepherds by saying: "For unto you is born this day in the city of David a Savior, who is Christ the Lord" (Luke 2:11).

TALK ABOUT IT

Why do criminals love darkness? Have you ever tried to hide something you did that was wrong? Why shouldn't we hide our sin? What should we do instead?

SING TOGETHER

The Christmas hymn for the week is "Hark! the Herald Angels Sing." The words were written almost 300 years ago by the famous pastor Charles Wesley. The words call us to join the angels in singing to the shepherds, "Christ is born in Bethlehem." Notice how the third verse contains the theme of light. Pastor Wesley wanted everyone to know that the baby Jesus came to bring light to all.

Hark! the Herald Angels Sing

Hark! the herald angels sing,
 "Glory to the new-born King!
Peace on earth, and mercy mild,
God and sinners reconciled."
Joyful, all ye nations, rise,
Join the triumph of the skies;
With th' angelic host proclaim,
"Christ is born in Bethlehem."
Hark! the herald angels sing,
"Glory to the newborn King!"

(SONG CONTINUES ON NEXT PAGE)

Christ, by highest heaven adored:
Christ, the everlasting Lord;
Late in time behold him come,
Offspring of the virgin's womb.
Veiled in flesh, the Godhead see;
Hail, th'incarnate Deity:
Pleased, as man, with men to dwell,
Jesus, our Emmanuel!
Hark! the herald angels sing,
"Glory to the newborn King!"

Hail! the heaven-born Prince of peace!
Hail! the Son of Righteousness!
Light and life to all he brings,
Risen with healing in his wings
Mild he lays his glory by,
Born that man no more may die:
Born to raise the sons of earth,
Born to give them second birth.
Hark! the herald angels sing,
"Glory to the newborn King!"

PRAY

Thank God for sending his son Jesus to be born in a manger on the very first Christmas. Ask him to shine his light in your heart so that every day you will turn from the darkness of sin and trust in him.

God's Rescue Plan

WARM-UP

SUPPLIES:

* paper

* crayons or markers

Read the Scripture for the day and have your children draw the baby Jesus held up by Simeon's hands in the center of their paper. Write the names of family, neighbors, and friends around the border. Then draw radiating lines in all the colors of the rainbow from Jesus in the center to each of the names. The radiating lines represent Jesus reaching all the peoples of the earth with his light and glory. Talk about how you might share this light with the names on the paper. One idea is to bake cookies and make Christmas cards to distribute to friends and neighbors.

READ THE WORD

Now there was a man in Jerusalem, whose name was Simeon, and this man was righteous and devout, waiting for the consolation of Israel, and the Holy Spirit was upon him. And it had been revealed to him by the Holy Spirit that he would not see death before he had seen the Lord's Christ. And he came in the Spirit into the temple, and when the parents brought in the child Jesus, to do for him according to the custom of the Law, he took him up in his arms and blessed God and said, "Lord, now you are letting your servant depart in peace, according to your word; for my eyes have seen your salvation that you have prepared in the presence of all peoples, a light for revelation to the Gentiles, and for glory to your people Israel." Luke 2:25-32

THINK ABOUT IT

God made a plan to send his only son into the world to be born as a man and die to take the punishment we all deserve for our sins. Then God's Son would lead his people out of the darkness of sin back into the light of God. For thousands of years the prophets spoke of God's plan to lead his people back into the light. Just as God spoke into the darkness and created light, God planned a "new creation" (2 Corinthians 5:17).

The prophet Isaiah revealed God's plan when he said,

The people who walked in darkness have seen a great light; those who dwelt in a land of deep darkness, on them has light shone. Isaiah 9:1-2

"I, the Lord, have called you in righteousness; I will take hold of your hand. I will keep you and will make you to be a covenant for the people and a light for the Gentiles, to open eyes that are blind, to free captives from prison and to release from the dungeon those who sit in darkness. . . . I will lead the blind by ways they have not known, along unfamiliar paths I will guide them; I will turn the darkness into light before them and make the rough places smooth. These are the things I will do; I will not forsake them." Isaiah 42:6-7, 16 NIV

Not long after Jesus's birth, Mary and Joseph brought him to the temple as the law required. A prophet named Simeon greeted them. He took baby Jesus into his arms and announced Jesus as the fulfillment of Isaiah's prophecy—"a light for revelation to the Gentiles, and for glory to your people Israel" (Luke 2:32). Put the two groups—Gentiles and God's people—together and we learn that God's salvation is for people of every nation. God had revealed to Simeon that he would not die until he saw the Savior God had promised—the One who would rescue God's people from the darkness of sin by shining the light of his salvation. So you see, Isaiah's prophecy is a foretelling of Christmas, the day Jesus, the Light of the World would be born.

And so God sent his son Jesus to be born and to grow up to be the one who would show all people the light of God. He first proclaimed the light of God's truth to the Jews. But sadly, most rejected Jesus. This is the apostle John's description: "The light has come into the world, and people loved the darkness rather than the light because their works were evil" (John 3:19). The Bible describes unbelievers as blind, saying: "The god of this world has blinded the minds of the unbelievers, to keep them from seeing the light of the gospel of the glory of Christ, who is the image of God" (2 Corinthians 4:4).

When the Jews refused to believe in Jesus, he reached out to those outside God's family—the Gentiles (for example, the Samaritan woman at the well)—and offered them salvation. After Jesus's resurrection and ascension, he called Saul (Paul) to be the apostle to the Gentiles and spread the light of the gospel to all people. This fulfills what the angel said to the shepherds, "I bring you good news of great joy that will be for all the people" (Luke 2:10).

TALK ABOUT IT

Why are the angel's words good news for "all the people"? Why are Simeon's words about how Jesus is a "light for revelation to the Gentiles, and for glory to your people Israel" (Luke 2:32) good news for all nations? Is there anyone left out of those two groups?

SING TOGETHER

Sing this week's Christmas hymn, "Hark! the Herald Angels Sing." (See p. 55.)

PRAY

Thank God for sending his only son Jesus on the first Christmas to be born into our world to save us from our sins.

Jesus, the Light of the World

WARM-UP

SUPPLIES:

* aluminum foil

* sharpened pencil

* permanent marker

* Styrofoam or sheet of cardboard

Write the word Jesus in large letters on a sheet of foil the size of a standard sheet of paper. Place the foil on top of the Styrofoam or cardboard and have the children poke holes in the foil along the letter outlines of the word Jesus. The holes will allow light to penetrate the foil.

Mount the foil on a lampshade. Cover the rest of the lampshade with foil. Tell your children that once it gets dark outside you will turn on the lamp.

When it is dark, gather your children and read John 8:12 where Jesus says, "I am the light of the world." Then turn on the lamp to see how the light penetrates through the perforations. Ask your kids, "Who is the light of the world?"

READ THE WORD

Again Jesus spoke to them, saying, "I am the light of the world. Whoever follows me will not walk in darkness, but will have the light of life." John 8:12

THINK ABOUT IT

The power of darkness was very strong, but Jesus broke it by living a perfect life and never sinning even once. Jesus healed the lame and gave sight to the blind; he forgave sins and even raised the dead. By these miracles he proved he had the power to push back the work of darkness. Jesus said,

"I am the light of the world. Whoever follows me will not walk in darkness, but will have the light of life." John 8:12

"As long as I am in the world, I am the light of the world." John 9:5

"I have come into the world as light, so that whoever believes in me may not remain in darkness." John 12:46

Jesus didn't say he was *like* light. Jesus repeatedly said, "I am the light."

When the Son of God stepped down from his throne to be born as a baby on the very first Christmas, he gave up his radiant glory (John 17:5) to be born a man (Philippians 2:7). Jesus did this so that he could live a normal life like you and me and experience the troubles and temptations we face. Though Jesus was tempted like us he never sinned. One day Jesus revealed his glorious light to three of his closest followers, Peter, James, and John. These men trusted Jesus and would later spread the news of his light. So Jesus "led them up a high mountain by themselves. And he was transfigured before them, and his face shone like the sun, and his clothes became white as light" (Matthew 17:1-2). These men would never forget what they saw.

Even though Jesus drew large crowds, most rejected him. The

powers of darkness led sinful men to betray Jesus, falsely accuse him, and nail him to a cross. There on that cross Jesus took the punishment for all the sins of those who would turn from darkness and call out for God to save them. Since Jesus was sinless, he could die in our place. There on the cross God the Father rejected his son and poured out on him the punishment we deserved. When Jesus bowed his head and died, darkness covered the land and it looked like the powers of darkness had destroyed all hope of the light.

But darkness did not win. God had planned for his son to take our punishment so that we could be forgiven. Death and darkness could not hold Jesus in the grave because Jesus had followed the law of God and obeyed God perfectly. Death and darkness had no claim on Jesus. On the third day, Jesus rose in victorious light, bright as lightning (Matthew 28:3). The light of Christ won a victory over the darkness of sin.

TALK ABOUT IT

What did Jesus, the Light of the World, do to overcome the power of sin and darkness?

SING TOGETHER

Sing this week's Christmas hymn, "Hark! the Herald Angels Sing." (See p. 55.)

PRAY

Thank Jesus for shining his light into our darkness. Thank him for showing us the truth and helping us to see that we are sinners who need Jesus to save us from the darkness of sin.

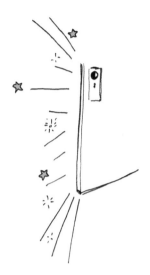

COME TO THE LIGHT

Light all the Advent candles before

reading chapter four of

"The Light Before Christmas"

and before each day's devotion.

☆ 4 ☆

SIGHT FOR THE BLIND

On the last Sunday before Christmas, Mia asked her grandmother, "So you were my age when you first read this book?"

Grandma replied, "Yes. My daddy loved to read, and each year for my birthday, he bought me a new book. This one has always been my favorite! We would read through these devotions every Advent season and finish on Christmas morning. If you look in the very beginning, you can read the inscription he wrote to me."

Mia quickly flipped back to the first page and read aloud: "My sweet girl, I pray that through this book, God will open your eyes to see the light of Christmas—the light of the gospel of the glory of Christ (2 Corinthians 4:4)."

"When I was young and first began reading the book," said Grandma, "I wasn't able to grasp the truths within its pages. But that changed over time."

"How so?" Mia asked.

"Well, to see and understand God's Word, we need the Holy Spirit's help. When Daddy first started reading to me, my heart was blind to the truth. By the time we finished, I could see."

"What did you see?"

"Everything. I saw the darkness of my own sin and how angry I was at God for not answering my prayers for healing. I had worked so hard to be good—in hopes that God would heal my eyes. But when he didn't, I grew bitter. That's when I told myself I would never follow him. I still went to church, but I wasn't at all interested. Yet over time, my heart began to soften. Eventually, God opened my eyes to believe, and everything began to change."

"How?" Mia asked.

"Well, I realized that I was a sinner in need of help. Apart from God showing me this—and giving me spiritual eyes to see—I wouldn't have recognized his great love for me. But I was able to see that he loved me enough to die for me. The Bible says that 'while we were sinners, Christ died for us' (Romans 5:8). This changed everything, including my prayer. Instead of asking God to heal my eyes, I asked him to help me see."

"Isn't that the same thing?" asked Mia.

"Yes and no," smiled Grandma. "Before that day, I tried pleasing God by doing good. I said I would only believe if he restored my sight. But when the Holy Spirit opened my heart to believe, I no longer needed to see with my eyes. My heart filled with joy and then I saw it—a vision of heaven and the brightest light you can ever imagine.

"Daddy stopped reading when a tear from my eyes dropped onto the book. He said that when he looked at me, my eyes were tightly closed, and tears were running down my face. A moment later, when

I opened my eyes, I was still blind—but inside my heart I could see.

"It was then that I truly believed that Jesus died for me on the cross and rose from the grave so that I could be forgiven. This filled me with a joy I had never known! My anger and bitterness melted away. It was the best Christmas ever! And it is why I love to sing,

"Shout joyful tidings, salvation has come,

The Light of Christmas in Bethlehem born.

The babe in a manger is God's only Son;

Good news of great joy, he is Christ the Lord.'"

"Did you ever see the vision of heaven and the light again?" Mia asked.

"Every time I read about light in the Bible, or hear the word light in a sermon, I picture God's bright throne. One day, when I see him face to face, my eyes will see what my heart believes. I will behold the glorious Son of God."

As contagious joy spread across Grandma's face, Mia became aware of the light in Grandma—a light that shone through darkness, drawing her near.

God's Mission: Bring People into the Light

WARM-UP

SUPPLIES:

* sheet of newspaper

* scissors

Tell your children the sheet of newspaper represents the good news of the gospel. Cut the sheet in half and explain that each time the paper is cut in half, it is like one person sharing the good news with one other person. Hold up the halves pointing out that now two people have the good news. Cut each half in half and explain that if both people each share with one other person, there are now four people who have the good news. If you keep doing this the Word of God spreads to a great number of people. Show how the 4 people become 8, then 16, then 32, then 64, etc.

If each of you were to continue sharing the gospel ten more times and everyone kept sharing you would have half a million Christians. That is how the light of the gospel spread throughout the world, simply by one person telling another.

If you haven't done it already, bake cookies and make Christmas cards to distribute to friends and neighbors. Plan on how to deliver them in person during the week. If you have a Christmas service at your church include a personal invitation.

READ THE WORD

Now the eleven disciples went to Galilee, to the mountain to which Jesus had directed them. And when they saw him they worshiped him, but some doubted. And Jesus came and said to them, "All authority in heaven and on earth has been given to me. Go therefore and make disciples of all nations, baptizing them in the name of the Father and of the Son and of the Holy Spirit, teaching them to observe all that I have commanded you. And behold, I am with you always, to the end of the age." Matthew 28:16-20

THINK ABOUT IT

Before Jesus returned to his Father in heaven, he told the disciples to pass on all he had commanded them (Matthew 28:20). Then Jesus ascended to heaven, promising to return again (John 14:1-3) to judge the earth (Matthew 16:27) and destroy those who walk in darkness (Matthew 25:41-46).

The disciples were instructed to wait for the promised Holy Spirit. While they were praying, tongues of fire appeared over each of them. The Spirit of God fell upon them. The Spirit of God helped them to remember all that Jesus taught them (John 14:26). From that point the disciples began to share the good news of the light.

John wrote about the light in his Gospel and spread the good news of the light through letters saying,

This is the message we have heard from him and proclaim to you, that God is light, and in him is no darkness at all. If we say we have fellowship with him while we walk in darkness, we lie and do not practice the truth. But if we walk in the light, as he is in the light, we have fellowship with one another, and the blood of Jesus his Son cleanses us from all sin. If we say we have no sin, we deceive ourselves, and the truth is not in us. If we confess our sins, he is faithful and just to forgive us our sins and to cleanse us from all unrighteousness. If we say we have not sinned, we make him a liar, and his word is not in us. 1 John 1:5–10

Still the darkness tried to put out the light. Unbelievers persecuted followers of Jesus. Saul (later called the Apostle Paul) was one of them. He arrested believers and had them killed. But God had a special plan for Saul. One day, on his way to the city of Damascus to arrest more Christians, Jesus appeared to Saul in a blinding light, brighter than the sun (Acts 26:13). Saul was knocked to the ground. When Saul asked who stood before him, Jesus replied,

"I am Jesus whom you are persecuting. But rise and stand upon your feet, for I have appeared to you for this purpose, to appoint you as a servant and witness to the things in which you have seen me and to those in which I will appear to you, delivering you from your people and from the Gentiles—to whom I am sending you to open their eyes, so that they may turn from darkness to light and from the power of Satan to God, that they may receive forgiveness of sins and a place among those who are sanctified by faith in me." Acts 26:15–18

That is why we must never change our greeting at Christmas from "Merry Christmas" to "Happy Holidays." The mission of Jesus

Christ began the day he was born and is the reason the angels rejoiced. When the skies opened to reveal the hosts of angels they sang "Glory to God in the highest" (Luke 2:14) not "Happy Holidays." Christmas is about God and the word "Christ" in Christmas tells us what the Christmas holiday is all about. It is all about Jesus.

TALK ABOUT IT

How can just one person sharing about Jesus make a big difference? How did the gift activity affect you? How did your sharing make a difference in the way you thought about the people you shared with?

SING TOGETHER

The Christmas hymn for the week is "O Little Town of Bethlehem." Pastor Philip Brooks wrote this song in 1868 for the children in Sunday school. The theme of light once again is found in this traditional hymn. An everlasting light pushes back the darkness with the coming of Jesus, born into Bethlehem.

O Little Town of Bethlehem

O little town of Bethlehem,
how still we see thee lie!
Above thy deep and dreamless sleep
the silent stars go by.
Yet in thy dark streets shineth
the everlasting light;
the hopes and fears of all the years
are met in thee tonight.

(SONG CONTINUES ON NEXT PAGE)

For Christ is born of Mary,
and gathered all above,
while mortals sleep, the angels keep
their watch of wond'ring love.
O morning stars, together
proclaim the holy birth!
And praises sing to God the King,
And peace to men on earth.

How silently, how silently,
the wondrous gift is giv'n!
So God imparts to human hearts
the blessings of his heaven.
No ear may hear his coming,
but in this world of sin,
where meek souls will receive him still
the dear Christ enters in.

O holy child of Bethlehem,
descend to us, we pray,
cast out our sin, and enter in,
be born in us today!
We hear the Christmas angels
the great glad tidings tell.
O come to us, abide with us,
our Lord Emmanuel.

PRAY

Ask God to help you share the gospel with others. Pray for the
friends and neighbors who received your gifts.

We Are the Light

WARM-UP

SUPPLIES:

* birthday candles
* index cards (one for each member of your family)

Cut the index cards in half and poke a hole in the center of each with the point of your scissors. Slide a candle into the hole. The card will serve as a drip shield to allow your children to hold a lit candle. Make one of these for each of your family to hold.

Talk about how we become a part of the light when we believe the gospel. When we share that message with others, we are sharing the light with them. Sing the traditional Christmas carol, "Go Tell It on the Mountain" with one parent's candle lit. Then one by one share the light until everyone has their candle lit. Note: If you do this with the lights off at night, it will add to the drama of the exercise.

Go, Tell It on the Mountain

CHORUS:

Go, tell it on the mountain,
over the hills and everywhere;
go, tell it on the mountain
that Jesus Christ is born.

(SONG CONTINUES ON NEXT PAGE)

While shepherds kept their watching
O'er silent flocks by night,
Behold, throughout the heavens
There shone a holy light. [Chorus]

CHORUS:
Go, tell it on the mountain,
over the hills and everywhere;
go, tell it on the mountain
that Jesus Christ is born.

The shepherds feared and trembled
When lo! above the earth
Rang out the angel chorus
That hailed our Savior's birth. [Chorus]

Down in a lowly manger
The humble Christ was born,
And God sent us salvation
That blessed Christmas morn. [Chorus]

READ THE WORD

[Jesus said,] "You are the light of the world. A city set on a hill cannot be hidden. Nor do people light a lamp and put it under a basket, but on a stand, and it gives light to all in the house. In the same way, let your light shine before others, so that they may see your good works and give glory to your Father who is in heaven." Matthew 5:14-16

THINK ABOUT IT

The apostles of Jesus passed on the message of the light of Christmas to those who would listen and believe. These new believers in turn passed on the message of the light to other people. And so from person to person and generation to generation the message of the gospel advanced. The Bible tells us that everyone who believes in Jesus comes into the light (John 12:46). Reread what Jesus said to his followers in today's Scripture above.

The Apostle Paul summed it up this way, "For God, who said, 'Let light shine out of darkness,' has shone in our hearts to give the light of the knowledge of the glory of God in the face of Jesus Christ" (2 Corinthians 4:6).

As has always been the case for followers of Jesus, it is our job to share his light. This fulfills the prophecy God gave to Isaiah:

"I am the LORD; I have called you in righteousness; I will take you by the hand and keep you; I will give you as a covenant for the people, a light for the nations." Isaiah 42:6

"I will make you as a light for the nations, that my salvation may reach to the end of the earth." Isaiah 49:6

Today we draw encouragement from what Paul taught the people of the early church:

For at one time you were darkness, but now you are light in the Lord. Walk as children of light (for the fruit of light is found in all that is good and right and true). Ephesians 5:8-9

That you may be blameless and innocent, children of God without blemish in the midst of a crooked and twisted generation, among whom you shine as lights in the world. Philippians 2:15

More than one hundred and fifty years ago the spiritual "Go Tell it on the Mountain" was written to capture the mission of God that began at the birth of Jesus. Today when people sing this lively song they shout the chorus with all their might and sway to the beat of the song as they sing.

Sing the song again, repeating the candle lighting if desired.

TALK ABOUT IT

What is the mission of Christmas? How does the song "Go Tell it on the Mountain" help us remember the mission of Christmas?

SING TOGETHER

Sing this week's Christmas hymn, "O Little Town of Bethlehem." (See p. 73.)

PRAY

Ask God to help each person in your family tell others about the true meaning of Christmas.

God's Light Will Shine Forever

WARM-UP

Sing the song, "This Little Light of Mine." Sing the lyrics below and add others that you might know. Remind your children that Jesus is the Light of the World and when we believe, we receive the light and are called to share it with others. One day in heaven Jesus will be our only light.

This Little Light of Mine

This little light of mine,
I'm gonna let it shine.
This little light of mine,
I'm gonna let it shine.
This little light of mine,
I'm gonna let it shine,
let it shine, let it shine, oh let it shine.

Ev'rywhere I go,
I'm gonna let it shine.
Ev'rywhere I go,
I'm gonna let it shine.
Ev'rywhere I go,
I'm gonna let it shine,
let it shine, let it shine, oh let it shine. (SONG CONTINUES ON NEXT PAGE)

Jesus gave it to me,
I'm gonna let it shine.
Jesus gave it to me,
I'm gonna let it shine.
Jesus gave it to me,
I'm gonna let it shine,
let it shine, let it shine, oh let it shine.

READ THE WORD

And I saw no temple in the city, for its temple is the Lord God the Almighty and the Lamb. And the city has no need of sun or moon to shine on it, for the glory of God gives it light, and its lamp is the Lamb. By its light will the nations walk, and the kings of the earth will bring their glory into it, and its gates will never be shut by day— and there will be no night there. They will bring into it the glory and the honor of the nations. But nothing unclean will ever enter it, nor anyone who does what is detestable or false, but only those who are written in the Lamb's book of life. Revelation 21:22–27

THINK ABOUT IT

One day Jesus will return to the earth with a shout and the sound of a trumpet (1 Thessalonians 4:16). On that day, we will all be changed (1 Corinthians 15:52). All our sickness and sorrows will be taken away and Jesus will judge all darkness and evil and sin (Revelation 22:12). He will cast Satan into the lake of fire (Revelation 20:10). All those who believe in the light will come into the radiant light of God and we shall look upon God face to face (1 Corinthians 13:12). We will see Jesus as he is (1 John 3:2). In heaven, God's people will live sin free, joy-filled lives (Revelation 21:4). We will worship God and enjoy him forever (Revelation 22:3).

Isaiah spoke of this day when he said,

The sun shall be no more your light by day, nor for brightness shall the moon give you light; but the LORD will be your everlasting light, and your God will be your glory. Your sun shall no more go down, nor your moon withdraw itself; for the LORD will be your everlasting light, and your days of mourning shall be ended. Isaiah 60:19-20

God will purify the earth with fire and make it new again with no darkness and no night. God will come down from heaven and live with his children in a great city. God will walk with his children as he walked with Adam and Eve in the garden before their fall into darkness and sin. There will be no need of the sun, for the glory of God will be our light.

John described this in the Book of Revelation:

And the city has no need of sun or moon to shine on it, for the glory of God gives it light, and its lamp is the Lamb. By its light will the nations walk, and the kings of the earth will bring their glory into it. Revelation 21:23-24

And night will be no more. They will need no light of lamp or sun, for the Lord God will be their light, and they will reign forever and ever. Revelation 22:5

While some stories have an end. This is the one eternal story that is never ending. We who reject the darkness of sin and put our trust in the light of Jesus will live with God forever and ever with no end (1 Thessalonians 4:17). God's call goes out to all people, young and old: Will you come out of the darkness of sin into the marvelous light of God? Will you trust and believe in Jesus, the Light of the World who was born a babe in a manger? Trusting in Jesus is the only way anyone can live forever in the light of God's presence. So now the call of God has come to you and you know the real meaning of Christmas Which will you choose, the darkness of sin or Christmas light?

TALK ABOUT IT
How does the Bible describe heaven? Why will we not need the sun for light in heaven?

SING TOGETHER
Sing this week's Christmas hymn, "O Little Town of Bethlehem." (See p. 73.)

PRAY
Ask Jesus to help you let your light shine and tell others about him.

CHRISTMAS CELEBRATION

Read the last chapter of the story on

Christmas Eve with four Advent candles

lit. On Christmas Day light all the

Advent candles and read the Scripture.

☆ 5 ☆

THE LIGHT OF CHRISTMAS

As Mia finished reading the last chapter in the book, she noticed Grandma's eyes again filling with tears. "Grandma, you're crying."

Grandma remarked, "These are happy tears, I promise! The Bible says that for a time, we see him in part, but one day we will see him face to face. Sometimes I imagine all the many people who will be there, and it floods my heart with joy! I want you to be there with me."

In that moment, Mia realized she had a decision to make. She always assumed she was a Christian because she went to church and knew the story of Jesus. But suddenly, God opened her eyes. She became keenly aware of her own sin, anger, and disobedience. She saw her own selfishness. Though she came to help Grandma, she realized that she also needed help. She needed God to open the eyes of her heart.

"Grandma, I want to see like you do—through the eyes of faith."

Grandma smiled, "The Bible says that when you trust in Christ's perfect life and sacrifice on the cross, God delivers you from darkness, and he moves you into the light."

"I believe, Grandma!" exclaimed Mia. "I want to walk in his light. What should I do?"

"Simply come! God welcomes you. He loves you, died for you, and conquered the grave for you. When you believe in this truth, it's finished! He's already done the work for you!"

"I believe, Grandma! I believe he has set all things right in my heart! I believe my sins are forgiven!"

"Then it is finished. You now walk in the light of Jesus! You are God's child—freely and fully forgiven—a child of the light."

Suddenly Mia began crying. Her grandmother wrapped her arms around her, drawing her near.

"I'm so thankful, Grandma," said Mia. "Thank you for sharing this book with me and for praying for me!"

Grandma responded, "It has been my joy and delight! How I've longed for this day! And now we can walk together in faith for all eternity."

After several minutes, Mia looked up and said, "I just imagined the throne of God! I saw it in my mind, Grandma. It was brighter than the sun. Oh, Grandma, I can't wait! One day we will both see with our eyes, face to face!"

Suddenly, there was a knock at the door. It was Mia's parents! Mia wiped her eyes and ran to the door.

"We've got a white Christmas," said her dad, stomping the last of the snow from his boots. Then he gave Mia a long, warm hug. We've missed you!" he said.

"How was your time with Grandma?" Mom asked.

"It's been wonderful!" exclaimed Grandma. "Take off your coats and come in. We've got a story to share. But first, you must be starved. I've got supper on the stove and a warm pie is cooling on the counter."

After dinner and dessert, Mia shared the story of reading *The Light Before Christmas* and all that God had done.

The next day at church, Pastor Jake greeted Mia and her family at the door. Mia asked if she could make a special Christmas hymn request. Pastor Jake smiled and said, "Of course! What would you like to sing?" he asked.

"Can we sing the song about the light?" she asked.

"It just so happens, it's already scheduled," smiled Pastor Jake. "I know it's one of your grandmother's favorites."

Later in worship, the choir filled the little brick church with loud rejoicing. The music shook the rafters, and spilled into the streets of the town. Long robes swayed as the choir danced and clapped their hands to the beat. Mia held her grandmother's hand tightly as they both sang with all their might:

I once lived in darkness, deep as the night,
Then God sent his Spirit to open my eyes.

The Light of the World gave me back my sight.
All heaven rejoiced when I saw the light.

Shout joyful tidings, salvation has come,
The Light of Christmas in Bethlehem born.
The babe in a manger is God's only Son;
Good news of great joy, he is Christ the Lord.

He will return, lock darkness away.
The light from his throne will light up our day.
Though brighter than sunbeams, we'll see face to face.
Forever forgiven, forever we'll praise.

Shout joyful tidings, salvation has come,
The Light of Christmas in Bethlehem born.
The babe in a manger is God's only Son;
Good news of great joy, he is Christ the Lord.

Christ Is Born!

SCRIPTURE READING LUKE 2: 1–20

In those days a decree went out from Caesar Augustus that all the world should be registered. This was the first registration when Quirinius was governor of Syria. And all went to be registered, each to his own town. And Joseph also went up from Galilee, from the town of Nazareth, to Judea, to the city of David, which is called Bethlehem, because he was of the house and lineage of David, to be registered with Mary, his betrothed, who was with child. And while they were there, the time came for her to give birth. And she gave birth to her firstborn son and wrapped him in swaddling cloths and laid him in a manger, because there was no place for them in the inn.

And in the same region there were shepherds out in the field, keeping watch over their flock by night. And an angel of the Lord appeared to them, and the glory of the Lord shone around them, and they were filled with great fear. And the angel said to them, "Fear not, for behold, I bring you good news of great joy that will be for all the people. For unto you is born this day in the city of David a Savior, who is Christ the Lord. And this will be a sign for you: you will find a baby wrapped in swaddling cloths and lying in a manger." And suddenly there was with the angel a multitude of the heavenly host praising God and saying,

"Glory to God in the highest, and on earth peace among those with whom he is pleased!"

When the angels went away from them into heaven, the shepherds said to one another, "Let us go over to Bethlehem and see this thing that has happened, which the Lord has made known to us." And they went with haste and found Mary and Joseph, and the baby lying in a manger. And when they saw it, they made known the saying that had been told them concerning this child. And all who heard it wondered at what the shepherds told them. But Mary treasured up all these things, pondering them in her heart. And the shepherds returned, glorifying and praising God for all they had heard and seen, as it had been told them. Luke 2:1–20

SING TOGETHER

Joy to the World

Joy to the world! the Lord is come;
Let earth receive her King;
Let every heart prepare him room,
And heaven and nature sing,
And heaven and nature sing,
And heaven, and heaven, and nature sing.

Joy to the world! the Savior reigns;
Let men their songs employ;
While fields and floods, rocks, hills, and plains
Repeat the sounding joy,
Repeat the sounding joy,
Repeat, repeat the sounding joy.

No more let sins and sorrows grow,
Nor thorns infest the ground;
He comes to make his blessings flow
Far as the curse is found,
Far as the curse is found,
Far as, far as, the curse is found.

He rules the world with truth and grace,
And makes the nations prove
The glories of his righteousness,
And wonders of his love,
And wonders of his love,
And wonders, wonders, of his love. ISAAC WATTS

PRAY

Thank God for sending his son Jesus to shine the light of God into the darkness of this world to open our blinded eyes to believe. If you are about to open gifts, ask God to help everyone remember that Jesus is the greatest gift of all.

COMPANION SUNDAY SCHOOL CURRICULUM

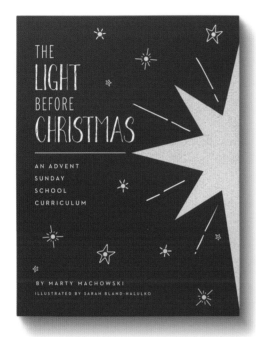

LESSONS INCLUDE

Week 1:
A Great Light in a Land of Deep Darkness
(Isaiah 9:2-7)

Week 2:
Jesus the Light of Men
(John 1:1-18)

Week 3:
Glory to God in the Highest
(Luke 2:1-20)

Week 4:
A Light to the Gentiles
(Luke 2:21-35)

The Light Before Christmas, a four-week Advent Sunday School curriculum by best-selling author Marty Machowski, guides children in learning about the reason we celebrate Christmas. Each lesson points to Christ, the Light of the World who came to save us from the darkness of sin. Through a Bible study of light and darkness, children will discover how the theme of light weaves its way through the Christmas story and God's plan of salvation.

This two-level (preschool and elementary) curriculum consists of lessons that include Scripture readings, dramas, object lessons, discussion questions, activity pages, crafts, and songs.

NewGrowthPress.com